Kuji-In for Ev

Ancient Spiritual Training
Adapted to our Modern World

F.Lepine Publishing

ISBN: 978-1-926659-07-7

www.KUJIIN.com

Table of Contents

Introduction

Mental Training Proven by Time

From the origin of time, men sought to refine their potential in every field. This natural interest in personal enhancement usually applied to physical attributes. It drove men to use every known technique to become stronger, faster, and more agile, especially in order to win competitions before audiences of admirers. In time, not only were the warriors and athletes competing, but in a subtler way, so too were the artists and the traders.

It has been known, mostly by professional athletes, that those who add mental training with their usual physical routine will obtain better results much faster than other than those who don't. Mental training can add the necessary edge to make a difference in the end, even for the most rigorous training regimen.

Mental training is naturally used as a reflex each time we are expecting to give all that we have, to perform, to go beyond our limits. Athletes, performers, and business people will take the time to concentrate and visualize their routine before every competition, match, event, show or presentation. They relax, breathe deeply and tell themselves that everything will be fine.

Imagine that this mental training was done consciously and in ways proven to be effective, rather than just intuitively. Imagine that instead of only practicing right before a crucial event, mental training was done before or after each training period, everyday, reinforcing what you already do best.

Although it seems completely off topic, there was a burst of movies in the 1980s that popularized the fighting styles, philosophies, and cultures of various martial arts disciplines. Among other things, there was often a mysterious technique that combined breathing, secret spoken words, and weird hand positions that seemed to put the warrior into a sacred state of mystical power. While it was unknown to the modern industrialized world, this technique has been used for ages by the Hindu, Chinese, and Japanese people. Aside from fighting and warfare, they used it in many fields of application: medicine, farming, religion, and business development. It just so happens that samurai used this technique to enhance their personal power, strength and fighting abilities, but were then portrayed in the movies in ways that made the practice seem even more mysterious.

The Japanese people called this technique *Kuji-In*, or "Nine Syllables", because of the nine spoken words. It also includes nine ways to place the hands, so it was named after the most obvious aspect of the "Nine Hand Seals". Kuji-In, which has been used for thousands of years as a means of self-empowerment, develops both the physical and mental potential of those who have the determination to study and apply it.

The "Nine Hand Seals" technique traveled through the ages in the cultural baggage of the various populations that used it. It was adopted as a meditation or religious practice, even a therapeutic dance. But once stripped of all dogma and belief, the original method can be useful to people from any culture, background, or profession. In the following pages, we will try to explain every aspect of the technique and how to use it in a modern, civilized world.

Self-empowerment is not simply a mental technique, but a process of transforming one's attitude in life. What you are now, is only what you know of yourself up to this point in your life, so a personal change is in order if you want to become more than that. The most important part of this ancient self-empowerment technique is the attitude change. You must study yourself as you are now and create a change for the better. Through this change in your character and personality, you will become more than what you are now: you will become Self-Empowered.

The beauty of the Kuji-In technique is that you do not have to use every component of it in order to benefit. For thousands of years, some traditional applications only used a few aspects of the technique, while others used all of them. If you feel uncomfortable with one or more aspects of the technique, feel free to use only the components that suit you. Some people only use this technique as a way to change their mental attitude.

In any case, as you develop the step-by-step tools explained in this book, you will feel the first results quickly and will notice more profound changes after more practice. You will feel energized, positive, and confident. Your doubts will give way to certainty and self-trust. Your body will regenerate faster and you will heal a bit faster than before. Most of all, your improved attitude towards life will be powerful and unshakable.

The Technique

Although the only apparent features would be the commonly seated posture while holding some kind of hand position, the Nine Hand Seals method actually combines five activities:

- a hand position
- a spoken expression
- a focus point in the body
- a mental visualization
- a philosophical concept to ponder

Some or all of these tools are used while breathing in a relaxed posture. The technique will reach its full potential when all five tools are used, but it is usually much easier to add elements one by one. For example, begin with two of the tools and add a third as you progress.

In this introduction to Kuji-In and Self-Empowerment, we wish to avoid inserting anything that would resemble the ancient religious or spiritual methods. It is a subject that may be studied separately if you are interested in a deeper understanding of Kuji-In, but we won't discuss it in detail here. The ancient spoken expression is a mantra, in Sanskrit, that contains esoteric wisdom.

The first step in Kuji-In training does not use the long Sanskrit mantra, but simply the recitation of a syllable, which is called a *kanji* in Japanese. For convenience, in our training we'll be using an English expression instead of this syllable. The spoken expression is not a translation of the Sanskrit mantra, but a philosophical adaptation of the kanji syllable (Rin, Kyo, Toh…) that is associated with each Kuji-In level. We will indicate the corresponding Sanskrit mantra for each level once you are acquainted with the basic Kanji technique.

When to Use

The technique can be used for a few minutes before any of your training or practice periods, or by themselves anytime during the day. We know of a few practitioners who use it for half an hour every day. It also works great right before you go to bed.

In time, practicing the technique will automatically put you in a state of relaxation and inner awareness. This will usually be at the cost of decreased awareness of your surroundings, but that is actually the goal. You will naturally generate your own mental cocoon when you practice, so it is necessary to warn you of an important side effect. If you start doing even a part of the technique while you are driving your car or doing something that requires your attention, you might get into this isolated mental state for a moment and put yourself and others at risk. It is often stronger than your will to drive carefully, so you would not like to use this wonderful technique and lose your concentration when it is most critical. We recommend you practice the Nine Hand Seals techniques in a suitable place for it, when your concentration is not required to keep you and other people safe.

This is not a technique to use while you are actually training or performing some other activity that requires your full attention, since it focuses your attention within yourself. Even though they will result in great benefits by themselves, the Nine Hand Seals assist your development by making your potential fully available when you need for training or practice. For this reason, an athlete must not use the Nine Hand Seals or its component tools while he is doing his actual routine. Instead, use the mental focus tools beforehand, when you are simply training in the gym. In the same manner, a musician will lose concentration if he tries to think about unrelated topics while also trying to play with efficiency. However, having practiced the Nine Hands Seals before, more neural connections will be available for him to benefit from his practice.

For example, the first technique (Step 1: Trust) is used to develop both physical strength and self-confidence. An athlete who practices enough of the first technique will have quicker results when bodybuilding, and faster recovery periods between each training. A businessman who takes the time to use the full technique 15 minutes each day for a week will feel much more comfortable when doing his presentations or holding negotiations.

Nerves and Meridians

The body is filled with nerves that carry electrochemical impulses, but it also has a subtler circuitry known as meridians. These meridians are commonly used in traditional Chinese medicine during the application of acupuncture. They are also the basis of some massage techniques since they have many beneficial influences on the mind and body. Their use normally induces a state of relaxation, making the body prone to recovery.

The hand positions cross and extend the fingers in ways to benefit from these meridians. Even though the meridians travel throughout the whole body, most start and end at the fingertips, thus the hand positions and finger puzzles. When you breathe while concentrating on focus points or acupressure points, it will work on these points in the same way an acupuncture needle or massage would.

In ancient India, the Hindu people tried every possibility: body positions, meditations, endless recitation of prayers, difficult fasting, and enduring many trials on their minds and bodies. It was a quest for the ultimate yoga of self-development. One of the legacies of these experiments was the use of hand positions that worked on the body and the mind in manners similar to what yoga would do, but were much easier to do than holding full body postures. The practice of using hand positions traveled to China and Japan along with the philosophy and meditation techniques.

Auto-Suggestion

The spoken expressions always represent a philosophy that we want to keep in mind and will accelerate the effects of the technique. It is known from the use of auto-suggestions and neural-linguistic programming that speaking can reinforce a concept, since it uses more parts of the brain to speak than if the idea is only contemplated. The important thing is to involve the brain in physical speech, so it does not matter which language is used. While many practitioners of Japanese Kuji-In appreciate speaking the Japanese words, a great many people also like to speak them in their mother language.

The concrete affirmations of philosophical expressions are a key component for mental training as it reinforces the concepts they represent in our mind. While repeating a few words that hold a certain meaning, the speech interacts with subconscious parts of our mind to make new connections and render the concept more accessible to our awareness, in our conscious mind. Although the spoken expressions used in our techniques might seem to differ a bit from the philosophical concept held in mind, their potential is used to its fullest since they work in combination with the mental concept. This entire aspect of auto-suggestion will become much simpler when you are finished learning the first technique.

Focus Points

When we pay attention to a place in our body for a long enough period of time, the focus point will become relaxed and our awareness of this place will be enhanced. Paying attention to a part of our body will accelerate its healing or regeneration since focused thought creates more neural activity in the parts of the brain relating to the area of attention. This extra energy is always used in the best possible way by the body. For example, people who use pain killers heal slower than those who do not because feeling pain continually attracts our attention to the injured area. While the time difference is not miraculous, it is notable. Each of our nine techniques requires us to focus on a specific point in the body not to heal it, but to enhance it. These focus points, specific to each of the nine techniques, are simultaneously a part of the meridian, nervous, and endocrine systems. They are also associated with an acupressure point, a main nervous centre, and a gland.

When focusing on a point in your body, it should be done with a relaxed attitude. It is not necessary to concentrate with force. Simply pay attention to the focus point and try to feel it. It might take quite a while before you feel any particular sensation at this focus point and it is not required. The technique will be enhanced the moment you pay attention to a specific place on your body.

Visualization

Visualization is an image that we imagine in our mind. Mental visualization is there to help us keep our attention on the technique and to prevent the mind from wandering too far astray. Do not pressure yourself to come back to the visualization if your thoughts stray, but do try to come back in a peaceful and relaxed way. Calmly reset the imagery in your mind.

The image kept in mind will assist with placing our attention on the focus point, but it will also use colours in ways known as chromotherapy (colour therapy). The psychological effect of the colour will enhance the efficiency of our practice period. Of course, the visualization itself will have a subtle reference to the philosophical concept held in mind.

Technique Introductions

Each of the nine methods will be introduced with a little explanation of its inner workings. Even though it is not required to understand all of these concepts for the techniques to work, it is recommended that you at least consider their meaning before you start combining the different tools.

Be forgiving with yourself while you are learning the first technique. Start by combining only two or three of the five recommended tools. Do not be stressed about the apparent complication of the method. All will come easily to you as you become more proficient with each step.

Step 1: Trust

Physical and Mental Strength

The goal of the first step is to aid the development of self-trust. This will give us the ability to drive more willpower in every action we undertake, resulting in a gain of physical and mental strength. When more energy is available to our nervous system when we need it, more energy also becomes available to our muscles in the deployment of physical force. In the same way, more mental energy will result in more strength of character, determination, perseverance, and courage.

This step is where we first pay attention to ourselves, thus we will use the concept of "meeting ourselves" in the spoken affirmation. The goal is to create and reinforce the contact we have with our inner self, with our body as well as our mind, so that every other aspect of the technique will be efficiently integrated.

We will contemplate the concept of "trust" and encourage ourselves to accept that we are capable of a great many things. We will loosen up our subconscious fears so that more of our precious energy can be given to the part of us that wants to expand in power and efficiency. In conjunction with creating a contact with our identity, it will also make more mental energy available to support every other action we take with willpower and determination.

Willpower is the ability to focus our will, an intense desire or aspiration, into a single accomplished feat. Yet our mind holds many secrets as to why we cannot give absolutely all the energy available when we apply willpower. It depends on many things: our mood, our state of mind, and even our feelings that day. All of this could be controlled and changed with reason - and will.

There are other aspects of ourselves that we cannot control so easily. For example, our brains do not always arrange themselves with all the optimal neural patterns to make all the energy available to accomplish an action. We also have those hidden memories and experiences that make our brains waste energy on poor neural connections and distribution.

For example, the body and the mind might remember the wounds of a training that did not go so well. It might focus on a performance that was unappreciated or judged poorly by others. Even the most self-confident people have these thoughts that nourish doubt, fear of failure, and even fear of pain. A part of the brain's energy is not used on the matter at hand, but rather is kept busy by these background thoughts.

Many times when people sense fear, feel threatened, or feel they are standing on unstable ground, the buttock muscles will tighten as a defensive reflex to protect an area called the "perineum". The perineum is the soft spot between the anus and sexual organs, right at the base of the body. It is a place where we identify the beginning and perpetuation of life. If this tender area is damaged, it might disrupt the functions of our nervous system. Despite this, it is a spot that we never pay attention to, thus the natural reactions we have are usually left to the subconscious mind and we seldom notice them. In this first exercise we will focus on the perineum. Paying attention to the perineum will simply make us aware of it and it will stimulate the free flow of energy in the area surrounding it. It will also help us become aware of our subconscious thoughts, or at least help us release ourselves of the subconscious control we keep on this area.

The Technique

Remember that you can start by using two of the five tools below, then add the remaining tools one at a time when you feel ready to progress.

The Concept

The concept we will ponder in this exercise is *self-trust*. In this form, you will repeat to yourself positive affirmations like:

- I accept myself
- I trust myself
- I have faith in my abilities
- I have all that it takes

Repeat these affirmations in your mind until the "unworded" concept of trust can be contemplated without the use of a worded reference. This means that we must try to hold the sense or feeling of it without actually repeating a phrases or reciting words mentally. This will let us reflect on self-trust without the use of a "spoken expression". Focus on the feeling of self-trust.

Hand position

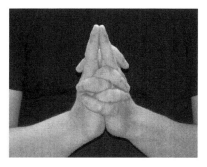

Extend your two middle fingers and interlace all other fingers. The photo on the left shows you how to keep your hands in front of you, at a level where you feel comfortable. The photo on the right shows you a side view to help you understand the finger placement in the hand position.

According to different systems, the middle finger has acupressure points to help augment the level of energy, treat fatigue, and regularize blood tension and circulation.

Spoken expression

The spoken expression associated with this technique is "I meet myself", which is inspired by the Japanese kanji RIN 臨. It should be spoken mentally only if you are unable to speak it out loud. The goal of this affirmation is to amplify the contact you have with your mental and physical systems- to amplify the attention that you give to yourself.

Of course you probably know who you are at the conscious level, but this affirmation will encourage you to make contact with the hidden parts of you that you probably do not know about. Another interesting side-effect of all our methods will be to help you eventually become aware of all that you are. This process starts with this first step, where you meet yourself in a subconscious, then conscious way.

Sanskrit mantra: Om vajramanataya swaha

Focus Point

We will focus on the perineum. We will simply pay attention to this point on our body, without using special effort or trying to feel anything in particular. Keeping our attention on this tender part of our body will help us re-create or encourage the contact we have with a physical, genetic part of us. It will also help us remain grounded and level-headed.

Mental Visualization

We will imagine that a red shining ball of light pulses at the level of our perineum. The red light is live activity, living energy, it is powerful, and it pulses softly, radiating red light. The ball can be 2-3 inches wide to start, but we will nourish it for a few minutes until it is big enough to surround our pelvis and coccyx area.

When you are about to finish this exercise, visualize the ball getting smaller again- not because it is getting weaker, but because it is concentrating all this accumulated red energy into the perineum. This last part can be done over a minute or for just a few seconds.

Example application:

2 tools: For a few minutes, hold the hand position and contemplate self-trust while breathing deeply and relaxing.

3 tools: For a few minutes, focus on your perineum while visualizing the red ball of energy radiating from there and recite "I meet myself".

5 tools: For a few minutes, contemplate self-trust, focus on your perineum while visualizing the red ball of energy radiating from there, hold the hand position, and recite "I meet myself". Breathe deeply and relax, and maintain all the aspects of the technique in focus.

For each step, feel free to use only the tools of the technique with which you feel comfortable.

Step 2: Responsibility

Self-Control and Free Will

This introduction will be the hardest to accept of all nine techniques, since it should awaken things that we try to bury deep inside our unconscious mind. Please read in a peaceful attitude and keep the self-trust from the previous exercise in mind.

The goal of the second step is to develop a conscious sense of responsibility and to "de-dramatize" the concept of consequence. Being in charge of our life is also being responsible for our actions, but the thoughts of consequences are too often associated with an emotion of guilt. Whatever the result of your actions, being responsible does not mean being guilty.

Each action we take has consequences. We are responsible of all the actions we take. This thought is terrifying to some people, yet it is inevitable. But why would such a simple concept be so frightening? There is a responsibility associated with drinking water and its consequence would be hydrating our body. Now, I do not see anything frightening in that! Too often is the concept of responsibility associated with punishment.

When some events turn out great, we may discard them or congratulate ourselves, but when something goes wrong we try to find who is responsible. This implies that the one responsible is the one guilty for what went wrong. Such a reaction is negative conditioning and reinforces the association that being responsible means being guilty.

Let us explain the difference between responsibility and guilt. Guilt is an emotion that we experience as the result of feeling persecuted or blamed. It often appears when someone is mad at us and, as it happens, other people are usually mad at us when we do something that has negative consequences for them. We may also feel guilty when we are mad at ourselves for taking certain actions, whether we are the cause of the event or not. We will feel guilt the moment we feel blamed, like when someone is mad at us. We might even feel guilty for the consequences of actions we did not take in the first place. Guilt appears when we believe that something is our fault, but it does not matter if it actually is our fault or not. Only the belief of culpability is required for guilt to manifest itself. This is one way that manipulative, or even abusive people, succeed in shifting responsibility to their victims. This is also how we play the game of being the victim of destiny, by simulating oppression from imaginary exterior sources.

Responsibility is the acknowledgment that the actions we take produce effects in the form of consequences or reactions.

Because of guilt, we tend to repress our sense of responsibility for a lot of events that had unhappy outcomes. Often, we have preferred to believe that these negative consequences were not the result of our actions, hoping that the emotion of guilt would subside. It can take quite a while for us to notice that repressing our sense of responsibility did nothing to stop the guilt anyway. Many people will never notice the difference. Thus, by denying that the actions we take have consequences, we implicitly affirm that we are powerless in our lives. And above that, we are still stuck with our emotions of guilt since we imagine that we do not have the power to relieve ourselves from it.

If we accept that our actions have effects in the form of consequences, then we also affirm that we have the ability to affect our lives and our environment. By accepting our responsibility, we are actually accepting that each time we were happy, when we felt good about ourselves, when we succeeded or accomplished something great, that it was in some way the result of our own doing- that we were responsible. Accepting our responsibility for what went wrong is also accepting our responsibility for what went right. Responsibility is accepting the consequences of all our actions and is not defined by the nature of the outcome. Responsibility implies that we have the means to operate changes.

By accepting that we are responsible for our actions, we affirm that we are powerful. Such a thought might have been impossible without self-trust, but this should not be a problem now that we have been through Step 1 (Self-Trust). You will come to notice how each step of the Nine Hand Seals affects the following steps. For now, simply believing in ourselves (Step 1) and admitting that we can affect our lives (Step 2) is valuable.

Another important aspect is the fact that you are in control of what happens to you, according to the actions you take. If you succumb to each of your emotional outbursts and justify your behavior by saying that it is not your fault, or that you cannot control it, then you are still affirming that you wish to bury yourself in guilt. This is an admission that you would rather be powerless than in control of your life. Sometimes it seems easier to delude ourselves into thinking that it is not our fault than to assume the responsibility of having strong emotions. Such belief would be a natural result of poor self-trust. But once you start developing self-trust, you will inevitably wish to become the master of your life again. In any case, we are still responsible for our actions even if we like to bury ourselves in guilt.

Whatever fantasy we build around our actions, whatever justification we invoke to feel more comfortable, we will always get from life what we put into it. Believing in being the victim of our unworthiness is a lie that resides only in our own mental conceptions of life. In truth, we are all already responsible and worthy of living a full life; we have only shielded ourselves from such beautiful affirmations of power due to our misunderstanding of the emotion of guilt. You might not be in control of a specific situation and you might not be responsible for certain events, but you are always in charge of how you react to it and what you can do to change the situation, especially if it affects your life.

Now, what should you do when guilt returns to camouflage your sense of responsibility? The first thing would be to take a deep breath and remind yourself that you are in charge of your experience. Then, accept the emotion without fighting it. Be aware of it and accept its presence in your guts. Try to revise the situation you are in and identify if you are "responsible" for the it or if you feel guilt because of misplaced self-blame. Do you have something to do with the situation? Can you change anything? This will help you work your way out of senseless guilt and into responsible free-will.

The Technique

For this exercise we will contemplate the fact that we are responsible for our actions, thus acknowledging our power to take control of our lives. Even if you do not yet believe this is possible, this exercise will progressively reconcile you with your right to take command of your life, to be in charge, to be responsible, and to know that you have the means to act accordingly.

The Concept

The concept we will ponder in this exercise is *responsibility*. In this form, you will repeat to yourself positive affirmations like:

- I am in charge of my life
- I am responsible for my actions
- I have the power to change
- I am free to act according to my will

Repeat these affirmations in your mind until the "unworded" concept of responsibility can be contemplated without the use of a worded reference.

Hand Position

Extend your index fingers and bend your middle fingers over your index fingers so that the tips of your thumbs are touching. Interlace all your other fingers. If you cannot touch the tips of your thumbs with your indexes, simply bend the middle fingers over the indexes as far as you can.

The index finger is correlated with the lower abdomen and is often used in acupressure to treat pains in this area. The thumbs have acupressure points affecting the throat, which relates to self-expression. In this hand position, we are combining the effect of returning our energy/tensions (middle finger) over our index finger which relates to the abdomen. Setting the complexity aside, we could resume this finger puzzle by saying that everything we do returns to us.

Spoken Expression

The spoken expression associated with the second technique is "Many means and methods" and is inspired by the kanji KYO 兵. It should be spoken mentally only if you are unable to speak it out loud. The goal of this affirmation is to condition yourself to believe that you have all the tools required to make your life what you want it to be.

At this point, tons of reactions from your mind may begin telling you that you do not have the means to take control of your life. These are normal reactions. They are the negative conditioning coming out. Do not pay attention to them, but also do not try to stop them. Simply continue with the exercise.

Sanskrit mantra: Om isha naya yantraya swaha

Focus Point

We will focus on the lower abdomen, in the area between our pelvis and our navel. This is where the guts are, where willpower expresses itself. It could explain why having "guts" means having willpower and courage. Simply focus your attention on this area.

Mental Visualization

We will imagine that an orange, sun-like shining ball pulses at the level of our lower abdomen. The orange sunlight is radiating outwards in every direction. It is powerful, but it pulses softly, radiating orange sunlight. The ball can be 2-3 inches wide at first, radiating orange sunlight in every direction, shedding light on everything.

Example Application:

2 tools: For a few minutes, hold the hand position and contemplate responsibility while breathing deeply and relaxing.

3 tools: For a few minutes, focus on your lower abdomen while visualizing the orange sunlight radiating from there and recite "Many means".

5 tools: For a few minutes, contemplate responsibility, focus on your lower abdomen while visualizing the orange sunlight radiating outward in every direction, hold the hand position, and recite "Many means". Breathe deeply and relax, and maintain all the aspects of the technique in focus.

Step 3: Harmony

Awareness and Tolerance

Now that you are building up your self-trust and developing a healthy sense of responsibility, it would be nice to learn how to be at peace in every situation. Being in control of your life does not always mean that you must always take action to change things. It takes some wisdom to identify when to act and when to let go. This is precisely the goal of this exercise.

We have normal, biological responses that encourage us to fight when we are faced with a conflict or threat. This has been a very useful survival mechanism for thousands of years, but it is not always useful or appropriate anymore. It would be nice to be relieved from this inner tension to fight, at least from time to time, so that we could find peace more easily.

However, we must first learn to pay attention to these reactions in order to identify them. We will be better able to decide how to respond if we take the time to perceive the rising anger, adrenaline, and stress of getting ready to defend our positions. If we are not paying attention, these impulses might simply take control of us and we could do something that we later regret. In fact, it becomes quite easy to say "I did not mean it" or "it was stronger than me". Yet you did nothing to stop yourself. Why is that? You simply were not paying attention to what was going on.

After so many years of reacting with these reflexive behaviours, it is normal to lose control of ourselves from time to time. It is not a behaviour that we can change in a few minutes. It is well anchored within us, both at the biologically and psychologically. Even so, we should not deny our responsibility (previous chapter) by saying that we could not stop ourselves. If we had trained ourselves at being aware of our inner defensive reactions, we would remember that we are responsible for our actions and that we have all the means necessary to take control of our lives.

To be at peace requires that we become aware of the inner fighting that occurs in times of stress and conflict. Notice what is fighting inside you. Where does the reaction come from? It usually comes from an area around the inner abdomen, where the anger usually takes its first form. Focusing on that tension will buy you precious seconds so that you can decide what to do with it, rather than just being overwhelmed by it.

When the pressure builds up, it is normal to want it to go away or to direct it outwards so that we can be relieved of it. Having a moment to decide what we will do gives us the chance to make better choices.

At this point, we encourage you to change your reactions into positive actions and to develop tolerance to what irritates you. This should not be done too quickly, so it is essential to practice at becoming aware of your inner fighting while you are not pressed by an irritating situation. In fact, we recommend you practice your inner awareness while you are calm and relaxed. This is in fact the goal of this third technique.

In a state of relaxation, pay attention to what is going on inside your inner abdomen. Whatever you feel, even if you do not feel a thing, you are slowly developing your inner awareness so that it will be available when you really need it. When you feel tensions and reactions rise from inside, try to adapt to it, instead of reacting to it. Try to accept its presence and let it be inside you, instead of doing all you can to push it outside. Give yourself permission to feel emotions instead of fighting your way out of the emotion. Allow the irritating feeling to remain for a moment, and breathe into it. The goal is to become fully aware of it. Once aware of the inner emotion behind any feeling, the pressure naturally lessens.

The Technique

We will now contemplate the fact that we are aware of our inner feelings and that we can remain calm and conscious, whatever the situation. We will practice at breathing into our abdomen to help our inner feelings reveal themselves. Do this technique mostly when you are calm and not experiencing any difficult emotions.

The Concept

The concept we will ponder in this exercise is *awareness and tolerance*. In this form, you will repeat to yourself positive affirmations like:

- I am aware of myself
- I accept what I feel inside
- I am at peace when I am aware
- I accept myself as I am

Repeat these affirmations in your mind until the "unworded" concept of inner awareness and tolerance can be contemplated without the use of a worded reference.

Knowing yourself is not intellectual. Applying the third step of self-empowerment will not reveal who you are in a tangible manner, but you will become aware of the abstract concepts that you subconsciously use to define yourself. In time, you will know yourself better even if you cannot put it into words.

Hand Position

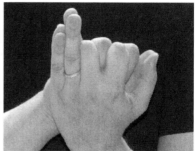

Point your thumbs and the last two fingers of both hands while keeping your index and middle fingers interlaced inside your hands.

The index finger is often used to point, to project outwards. The middle finger is the main finger used to operate our daily hand movements. Both these fingers are now turned inside the hands, and it helps get in touch with our inner feelings. Only the two smallest fingers stand out, which represent subtlety and sensitivity.

Spoken expression

The spoken expression associated with the third technique is "Who am I?", which is inspired by the kanji TOH 闘. It should be spoken mentally only if you are unable to speak it out loud. The goal of this affirmation is obvious. It is aimed at triggering the discovery of what you are inside by asking yourself directly. The question should not be followed by an improvised answer. You should simply pay attention and accept whatever rises from inside. It often happens that emotional reactions rise from within when we do this for the first few times. This is normal, but you should try to calm these reactions rather than encourage them.

In the previous exercise (Step 2), the reactions tended to come from your mind. This time the reactions may be a bit more emotional, but this is positive. This third step releases inner pressure that you unconsciously keep inside, which will provide you with more energy and freedom of action afterwards. Breathe deeply when you practice each technique. Some people tend to play a role of "victim" when they feel emotions. Try not to give into this type of behaviour. This technique aims to free you, not to encourage the same patterns that failed you in the past.

Sanskrit mantra: Om jita rashi yatra jiva ratna swaha

Focus Point

We will focus on the inner abdomen, so that the contact will be easier to make with your subconscious self. Pay attention to the area inside your guts and bowels. Relax your abdomen.

Mental Visualization

We will migrate from the previous orange sunlight outside our abdomen to a yellow-golden sun that emits light inside our body. We try to spread light inside our emotional centre and release the knots and clogs that are there. See the light flow freely inside your body.

Example Application:

2 tools: For a few minutes, hold the hand position and contemplate awareness while breathing deeply and relaxing.

3 tools: For a few minutes, focus on your inner abdomen while visualizing the yellow-golden sunlight radiating from there and ask yourself "Who am I?"

5 tools: For a few minutes, contemplate awareness and tolerance, visualize the yellow-golden sunlight ball shining from your inner abdomen and throughout your entire body, hold the hand position, and ask yourself "Who am I?" Breathe deeply and relax, and maintain all the aspects of the technique in focus. Accept the sensations and feelings that come out, but neither encourage nor disregard them. Be as impartial as possible and accept what is revealed from inside you.

Step 4: Power

Affirmation and Determination

Only once you are aware of who you are can you start affirming yourself. Any other type of personal affirmation is but theatre and perhaps even a desperate attempt to gain more attention or importance. Again, knowing yourself is not obvious at the intellectual level, but is instead a feeling of who you are and how you define yourself. Beyond that, nothing prevents you from changing your definition of self the moment you start being aware of who you are.

The fourth technique consists of harnessing the feelings of "Self" that you have discovered so far, and investing them in action, energy and movement. It is the expression of personal power to its fullest. This is what you have been working on since the first step of this series of exercises.

In order to develop true self-empowerment, you first had to trust yourself (Step 1). Then you had to re-acquire the knowledge that you have the power to affect your environment (Step 2). This is developed by accepting that you are responsible for your actions, which confirms that the actions you take have an actual effect on both you and your environment. With the first two steps you have developed the attitude it takes to empower yourself. Now, what fuels self-empowerment is… the Self! The mental and emotional awareness that you progressively develop with the third step is exactly what fuels your self-empowerment. With this subtle link to your "Self", you can now express yourself outwardly with more trust, responsibility, and awareness.

Self-empowerment changes your life for the better. In every action you take and every word you speak, you will be more confident in yourself. But self-empowerment has nothing to do with imposing yourself on your environment or others. Personal power has nothing to do with conflict or domination. When you know who you are and feel confident, you do not need to take more space than required, nor do you need to pressure others.

Do not try to project this power outwardly onto other people. Doing this would only reveal the insecurity that remains inside you. The actions you take should be done with energy and determination, but this should not be used to influence other people. Being infused with self-power makes it easier to offend other people. Remember that you are responsible for your actions and that by feeling filled with yourself, trusting and confident, you might forget that people around you are more sensitive to your actions. The challenge of the fourth step of self-empowerment is to be filled with your Self as an individual, but to do so without developing arrogance. Stay focused on yourself and continue developing self-trust and responsibility. You are encouraged to defend yourself when attacked, but never to attack first.

Along with the development of this new power from within, you will see more and more changes in your environment. People will react differently to you and you will be less influenced by attacks and conflicts. You will develop the means to make your life better… or worse. So you might as well act in ways to create a wonderful life for yourself and the people around you. The more you smile, the more people will be happy to be with you.

Self-empowerment will also have certain side-effects in your body. You will be able to solicit more electricity from your brain and nervous system, back into your muscles, thus becoming progressively stronger. You will have access to more energy and your body will find it easier to recuperate after a physical effort. In time even your body will heal wounds quicker and you will fight sickness with more ease.

The Technique

This is the place to take command of yourself, but not by over-stressing your body with strength. If you notice you are contracting your muscles, especially the abdomen, then you are not in a state of self-empowerment. This is instead a state of control that will only hinder your development of personal power. Relax and feel the power come from within. Most of all, trust yourself.

The Concept

The concept we will ponder in this exercise is *determination and perseverance*. In this form, you will repeat to yourself positive affirmations like:

- I am determined and perseverant
- I have the power to act
- I am at peace when I am in power
- I am the master of my life

Repeat these affirmations in your mind until the "unworded" concept of determination and perseverance can be contemplated without the use of a worded reference.

Hand Position

Extend your thumbs, index fingers and both little fingers. Interlace your middle and fourth fingers inside your hands. With this hand posture, we are pointing outwards with our index finger, the finger of affirmation. We are also keeping the finger of sensitivity out, the little finger. The thumb is the finger of support and expression.

Spoken Expression

The spoken expression associated with the fourth technique is the answer to the previous question: "I AM", which is inspired by the kanji SHA 者. It should be spoken mentally only if you are unable to speak it out loud. When you utter aloud or silently that "I AM", you should not try to define who you are, but simply let the conceptual feeling of Self (developed in Step 3) fill you up in a relaxed and positive manner.

Sanskrit mantra: Om haya vajramanataya swaha

Focus Point

We will focus on the solar plexus, which is the soft spot below your sternum. The solar plexus is an important nervous centre that has white and gray nervous matter, similar to the brain. In the brain, the gray matter helps us understand the outside world and the white matter helps us feel what is going on inside. Yet in the solar plexus, the white matter is on the outside and the gray matter is inside. Thus, the solar plexus is the centre where we feel what is going on outside and understand what is going on inside.

Mental Visualization

The yellow-golden sunlight developed in the third technique will now fill our body and express itself outwardly from our solar plexus. At this point, the solar plexus should radiate intensely from within to shine everywhere around us.

Example Application:

2 tools: For a few minutes, hold the hand position and contemplate determination while breathing deeply and relaxing.

3 tools: For a few minutes, focus on your solar plexus while visualizing the yellow-golden sunlight radiating outwards from there and say to yourself "I AM".

5 tools: For a few minutes, contemplate determination and perseverance, focus on your solar plexus while visualizing the yellow-golden sunlight radiating outwards from there, hold the hand position, and say to yourself "I AM". Breathe deeply and relax, and maintain all the aspects of the technique in focus. Do not supress or judge the feeling of what you are. Accept how you will reveal yourself to yourself. Let the technique work on you and you will naturally develop self-empowerment.

Step 5: Worth

Deserving Self-Empowerment

Another hindrance to the development of self-empowerment concerns the idea of "self-worth". The definition of our personal self-worth may be troubled by unknown or forgotten past experiences, often for the same reasons we lack self-trust. Although we might trust in our ability to accomplish something, we might also not believe we are worth it. As before, this reserves a part of our mental energy for self-judgment and denigration. Even without treating the cause of poor self-worth, we can still make a conscious effort to quiet our self-judging and harmful internal monologues. Now that we have increasing self-trust, it will be much easier to focus on positive thoughts and release from our subconscious mind a part of the limiting negative conditioning.

While you are working on changing your attitude towards life, you are invited to pay attention to the way you express yourself and how you perceive life. Are you more positive? Are you more negative? Do you play an ego game of being the victim of whatever happens to you? Do you have unresolved guilt that leads you to believe you are not worth the effort?

While it is not the goal of this book to provide emotional therapy, you are encouraged to work on forgiving yourself for whatever keeps guilt inside you. Guilt negatively influences your sense of self-worth and serves no other goal than your own destruction.

Do all that you can to keep a positive attitude towards life. Use the bad luck and failures to focus on bettering yourself and turn them into fuel for positive change. If you tend to complain about everything, try to hold yourself back from wasting this precious energy and instead focus on appreciating what you have.

The Technique

The concept of self-worth will slowly be reprogrammed in your thought processes as you practice the following technique. Do not be discouraged when you see a lack of results after only a few tries. Keep your determination and perseverance up and, most importantly, believe in yourself.

The Concept

The concept we will ponder in this exercise is *deserving happiness*. In this form, you will repeat to yourself positive affirmations like:

- I deserve to be happy

- I am positively powerful
- I am complete when I am happy
- I am a complete being

Repeat these affirmations in your mind until the "unworded" concepts of happiness and wholeness can be contemplated without the use of a worded reference, even if you do not actually feel the emotion of happiness.

Hand Position

Interlace all of your fingers, with the tip of each finger pressing into the root of the facing finger.

With all fingers joining together, you are affirming that you are a complete being, where all components work together. Nothing is missing.

Spoken Expression

The spoken expression associated with the fifth technique is a continuation of the previous affirmation: "I am complete", which is inspired by the kanji KAI 皆. Again, when you utter aloud or silently that "I am complete", you should not try to define who you are, but simply let the conceptual feeling of Self and wholeness fill you up in a relaxed and positive manner.

Sanskrit mantra: Om namah samanta vajranam ham

Focus Point

We will focus on the heart, the physical centre of self-worth.

Mental Visualization

The yellow-golden sunlight developed in the third and fourth technique will now fill your heart with warmth. You should also visualize a glowing sphere appearing around your entire body, radiating blue energy.

As you practice this fifth step, remember all the other techniques by reminding yourself that you trust yourself more and more everyday. You are responsible for your actions and you have the means to change your life. You are peacefully accepting who you are now, while still focusing on changing your life for the better.

You are self-empowered, powerful yet peaceful. You are worth it and you deserve to be a happy, complete being.

The remaining steps, from 6 to 9, are more abstract than the others. They will work on your subconscious mind to free the mental processes that hinder your self-empowerment. They will contain much less explanations, but they will be a great support to what you have developed up to now.

If you want to learn more about these steps, you will need to embark on a spiritual path. Whether guided by a competent teacher or traveled on your own, there must be a conscious spiritual path. It must also be a serious spiritual process with determination in the practice of the technique. Every spiritual technique is just fun to know, but will not bear any fruits without practice. Knowledge is essential, but only experience will bring wisdom and experience requires practice. You can't think experiences, you can only experience experiences.

I personally know someone who says that he never did any of the spiritual practices, and yet he experienced high states of spiritual bliss, but he did spent time everyday to look at himself, for personal growth purposes. Every day he took time to ponder his experience, breathe into his emotions, and observe his ego/mind at work. It doesn't seem like it, but introspection can be an effective spiritual practice. It would be wise to broaden your perception of what a spiritual practice is, and spirituality as a whole.

Step 6: Understanding

Enhancing Mental Processes

Things are not always as they seem and sometimes we simply do not understand things as they are. The purpose of this technique is to let go of the limits we place on the ways we think. The more you practice this step, the better able you will be to understand the nature of things. You will also learn new concepts in any area more quickly.

The Technique

This technique aims at developing the fluidity and efficiency of the mental processes. It allows us to better manage our ability to understand and express ideas.

The Concept

The mental concept to be pondered:

- My mind is free
- My mind is clear

Hand position

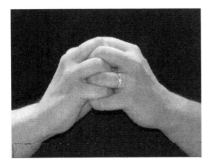 

Interlace all your fingers with your fingertips inside, each of them touching the equivalent tip of the other hand's finger, if possible.

With all fingers joining together inside the hands, we try to access the various links we make in our mind.

Spoken Expression

The spoken expression is: "I understand", which is inspired by the kanji JIN 陣. Understanding is more than intellectual computation or knowing definitions, but there is not much else to say at this introductive level. We will discover more about JIN in the advanced Kuji-In studies.

Sanskrit mantra: Om agnaya yanmaya swaha

Focus point

We will focus on the base of the throat.

Mental Visualization

Focus on the blue sphere around your entire body, glowing with radiating energy.

Step 7: Perception

Enhancing Perception

Things are not always as they seem, and sometimes we simply do not perceive them as they are. The purpose of this technique is to let go of the limits we place on our perception of the world, but it is not always easy to understand this concept intellectually. To better understand the phenomena of perception, we recommend that you read "Broaden Your Perception" by Simon Lacouline, ISBN 978-1926659039.

The Technique

This technique aims to develop your ability to perceive things from more than one angle at a time.

The Concept

The concept to be pondered:

- My eyes are free

- My ears are free

- My perception is free

Hand Position

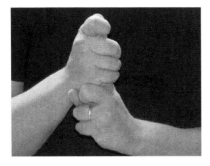

Point your left index finger up. Wrap the fingers of your right hand around your left index finger. Place the tips of your right thumb and index finger in contact with the tip of your left index finger. The fingers of your left hand are gathered into a fist. This hand position connects multiple pressure points related to eyesight, perception and mental processes.

Spoken Expression

The spoken expression is: "Many levels", which is inspired by the kanji RETSu 列. This kanji means "dimension" or "split".

Sanskrit mantra: Om jyota-hi chandoga jiva tay swaha

Focus Point

Focus on the pointy bone at the base of your skull.

Mental Visualization

The blue sphere around your body turns white and splits into two spheres. One sphere grows wider around your body while the other becomes smaller to fit your body's shape.

Step 8: Creativity

Stimulating Creativity

Our creativity depends on our ability to imagine new concepts, but it is not limited to artistic competence. It is useful when we make life-changing decisions and also, on a less dramatic level, when we find solutions to everyday problems. Creativity can help us decide little things like which products will best suit our needs or which roads we will use to get somewhere.

Many parts of the brain are involved in creativity. This step of the technique helps the different parts of your brain work together harmoniously, in order to make creativity more accessible.

The Technique

This technique aims to develop your creativity.

The Concept

The concept to be pondered:

- I am creative
- My imagination is free

Hand Position

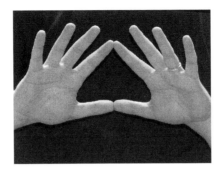

Touch the tips of your thumbs and index fingers to form a triangle, while your other fingers are spread out.

Spoken Expression

The spoken expression is: "Everything, everywhere", which is inspired by the kanji ZAI 在.

Sanskrit mantra: Om srija iva rutaya swaha

Focus Point

Focus on centre of your forehead at the upper bridge of the nose.

Mental Visualization

Everything turns to white, everywhere.

Step 9: Peace

Become at Peace

The most abstract and simple step of the technique consists of a final relaxation at the end of the entire process. This step of the technique will do more than relax you. It will keep your nervous system healthy, which will have an impact on the whole of your being.

The Technique

This technique aims to set you at peace. Try to relax as much as possible. You may pass out during this step, but this is completely acceptable. You are not going to sleep, but your nervous system enters a state that we call transcendence.

The Concept

The concept to be pondered:

- Everything is simple
- Everything is perfect

Hand Position

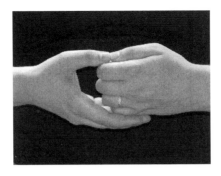

Rest your left knuckles on the fingers of your right hand, with your right palm open. Touch the tips of your two thumbs gently.

Spoken Expression

The spoken expression is: "Perfection", which is inspired by the kanji ZEN 前.

Sanskrit mantra: Om arapacana dhi

Focus Point

Focus on the entire upper portion of your head.

Mental Visualization

Now that everything is white, softly let go of any visualization.

Conclusion

Self-Empowerment

Self-empowerment is not simply the feeling of a power-trip. It is a true step forward in your personal development. It should be used for the sole purpose of becoming better at everything you do. Take some time each day to do this wonderful technique and you will enhance your entire experience. Do not be afraid to confront yourself and change your attitude.

Now that you have gone through all the steps of the technique and learned them one by one, try to apply each step. Do them in order and practice each one for a few minutes. If there is one aspect of the technique you wish to develop more, simply spend more time on this technique and less on the others. Yet, because each technique is linked with the previous one, it is important for any of the techniques to work that all of them be practiced, even if for just a little while.

Good luck with your practice. If you ever have any questions, please feel free to browse our web site at **www.kujiin.com** and contact any of the certified teachers.

MahaVajra

Kuji-In for Everyone

Ancient Spiritual Training
Adapted to our Modern World

F.Lepine Publishing

© François Lépine, 2006
ISBN: 978-1-926659-07-7

www.KUJIIN.com

25696783R00042

Printed in Great Britain
by Amazon